Given to

_____

From

_____

_____

# Of Gardens & Grandchildren

## Reflections on Love and Life

## Brian Kelley Bauknight

**DIMENSIONS**

FOR LIVING

NASHVILLE

## OF GARDENS AND GRANDCHILDREN
### Reflections on Love and Life

### Library of Congress Cataloging-in-Publication Data

Bauknight, Brian Kelley, 1939-
    Of gardens and grandchildren : reflections on love and life / Brian Kelley Bauknight.
       p.     cm.
   **ISBN 0-687-28423-6 (alk. paper)**
    1. Meditations.   2. Bauknight, Brian Kelly, 1939—Family.
   3. Bauknight family.   4. Vegetable gardening—Meditations.
   I. Title.
BV4832.2.B345     1993
242—dc20                              92-33158
                                           CIP

Scripture quotations are from the New Revised Standard Version of the Bible, copyright 1989 by the Division of Christian Education of the National Council of the Churches of Christ in the U.S.A. Used by permission.

MANUFACTURED IN THE UNITED STATES OF AMERICA

*For Matthew Stephen*
*Andrew Brian*
*Casey Marie*
*Luke Thomas*

*and others yet to come,*
*who have brought new wonder and joy to my life*

# Contents

Introduction   7

A Catalog of Promise   9

Sensory Bombardment   11

Improving with Age   13

Special Delivery   15

Choosing the Top Bunk   18

Back-ordered   20

Unafraid   22

Clay Pots   24

Broccoli with Cheese   27

Iced Crocus   30

From Brown to Green   32

Simultaneous Stretching   35

Leaning on the Everlasting Arms   37

Kentucky Wonder   39

Fast Food Convenience   41

Safari Adventure   43

Bare Necessities   45

The Big Puddle   47

A Priceless Invitation   50

The Home Run   52

Forehead   55

A Working Definition   *57*

Savvy Christians   *60*

A Singing Irony   *62*

To Be a Child Again   *64*

Declaration of Interdependence   *66*

Inaugural Wonder   *68*

Small-scale Soil Erosion   *70*

Twice Blessed   *72*

Clapping and Praying   *74*

Time to Do and Be   *76*

Dinosaur Bones   *78*

Putting the Yard to Bed   *81*

Knowing When to Point   *83*

The Missing Puzzle Piece   *85*

Useless Growth   *88*

The Legacy of the Three Little Pigs   *90*

Yes! And Amen!   *92*

The Cycle Continues   *94*

About the Author   *96*

# Introduction

For much of my adult life, a favorite hobby has been a home vegetable garden. Please understand that it has never been a big thing in terms of acreage. I am certainly no farmer in suburbia. My garden has consisted of only a few hundred square feet. But I have found some great joy, healthy exercise, good nutrition, and a genuine sense of escape in the garden.

Over the years, this hobby has necessitated the purchase of a tiller, a shredder/mulcher (in two sizes), a variety of hand tools, an interesting array of gardener's gadgets, and a good supply of home canning and freezing equipment. Just how much money has actually been saved in the family food budget over the years is quite indeterminable. Probably not much. But the garden is my pet project and a loving diversion in an ever-expanding growing season. From time to time, I also have found in the garden a few parables about love and life—about growth along the Christian journey.

In recent years, my life has changed in innumerable ways. Primarily, however, a new distraction has entered my life: grandchildren! First came one grandson (Matthew). Then, two (Andrew). Then, with the remarkable good sense to be born on my own fifty-first birthday, a beautiful granddaughter (Casey)! As this is written, another little person (Luke) has entered the world.

These precious little people have lifted my spirits, taxed my energies, commanded my attention, and focused my love in very special ways. Moreover, they have provided a fair number of marvelous parables and images of their own for the inevitable twists and turns of the Christian journey. To some extent they are now old enough to help in my garden. The mixture of garden and grandchildren has been one of immeasurable joy.

So—with appreciation to my wife, Elaine, for her indulgence of my gardening hobby; with appreciation to Matthew, Andrew, and Casey for their unending supply of antics and profound images; and with appreciation to my congregations who have put up with a lot of stories about both—I offer this little book. As a guide to devotional reading, each parable is referenced to some brief word of Scripture. In some fashion, the order of the parables follows the path of the calendar year and the various seasons of the Christian faith.

Parables are everywhere. Jesus made parables work in memorable stories and images which have endured. My prayer is that some of these might endure as well. Together, people of faith have always sought simple metaphors and loving portraits of what it may be like to be on the adventure of the spiritual journey. Here are a few for the living of these days.

# A Catalog of Promise

Faithfully, predictably, it arrives at the same time each year—in the days between Christmas and the dawn of the New Year. On a cold, wintry day comes the seed catalog for the seemingly distant spring.

The cover and inside pages glisten with colorful guarantees. Bright, shining eggplant (without blemish or discoloration), fully ripened tomatoes (with morning dew droplets hanging on each firm succulent sphere), and perfectly shaped bush beans (hanging straight and unsoiled from uniformly healthy plants). There is never a weed, an aphid, a broccoli worm, or a squash bug in sight.

Each year's new catalog is a symbol of God's covenant with humanity. Spring will come. The warmed, well-mulched soil will produce its fruits. The earth will be green and lush once again.

God wants us to hear the same promise in the midst of each "winter" of our lives. To do anything less is to betray that which God has planted within us. More than any other religious tradition, Christians are a people of indomitable hope.

Even when our lives seem bleak and hold no spark of joy or assurance, God extends the guarantee to uphold us. The strong right hand of God will not fail us. God will see us through into the season of growth once again, and we will experience the fruits of the Spirit in our lives.

Leafing through the seed catalog, preparing to place an order for another spring, I am reminded of the constant image and messages of great promise everywhere in the gospel. Such promises, rightly received, will never disappoint us.

# Sensory Bombardment

*In him was life, and the life was the light of all people.*
*The light shines in the darkness, and the darkness did*
*not overcome it. (John 1:4-5)*

I t was a few days after Christmas. Matthew and I were playing with a few of his new toys in the middle of the living room floor. He asked me to assist him with the first try at a new puzzle he had received as one of his gifts. I heartily agreed, and we lay on the floor together. Matthew began the systematic search for outside pieces and matching color combinations. He was doing quite well for someone just over two years of age.

As we lay on the floor together, I suddenly became aware of the multitude of other inputs which came from the area around us. Directly in front of us, the television was broadcasting a children's television special. To the right, a Big Bird tape player was playing a song, with the beak of the Bird moving up and down in synchronization with the words to the song. And to the left was some kind of double-looped, battery-operated dolphin track chirping a poor imitation of dolphin sounds.

Matthew seemed oblivious to the barrage of noises around us, even though the combination of inputs seemed far more intense than those of his mother's generation years earlier. I could not help wondering if what we were experiencing was not a descriptive parable of life as we now know it. It is not easy to put together the pieces of the puzzle of life today. The puzzle is more complex than ever, and requires care, attention, illumination, and thoughtful reflection. Meanwhile, the world keeps moving in on us, encroaching slowly but steadily. The multiple inputs of our daily life are growing constantly, and exposure to the Light diminishes. How do we sort it all out? How do we maintain our focus upon the primary construction of life's essential picture with so many distractions, so many issues to deter and dissuade us from our intended purpose?

May God grant us enough courage to slowly shut down the nonessentials, at least for a time, so that we can rediscover who we are and Whose we are in the grand design of God's eternal purpose. May God grant us the Light that outshines any darkness.

# Improving with Age

> *I pray that the God of our Lord Jesus Christ, the Father of glory, may give you a spirit of wisdom and revelation as you come to know him. (Ephesians 1:17)*

One year, my Christmas present from our grandchildren was a very large, brightly colored sweatshirt. In bold, almost garish lettering across the front, it read: "Super No. 1 Special Grandpa." (I liked that part!) Then, below, in somewhat smaller lettering were the added words, "Improves with age!"

I reflected upon the message and its meaning as I wore the sweatshirt for a few hours that Christmas season. In the casual comfort of several chilly December days, two thoughts came to mind.

First, it is certainly true that age can produce wisdom. (Wisdom is not guaranteed, of course!) The biblical witness is fairly consistent on this point.

Life experiences and an accumulation of life events teach us a great deal. We learn not to take ourselves too seriously. We learn to value friendships and family ties. We learn that life is too short to harbor anger or resentment, not to mention the attendant risks of health problems as a result of unresolved anger. We learn to be childlike once again. We learn to modify our desire for accumulated things, and to cherish memories.

I believe that some of the most beloved of the Psalms of the Old Testament were composed and written by persons who could look back upon life with the profound wisdom of many accumulated years. Perhaps David wrote Psalms as a man of mature years, or perhaps he wrote them as a young boy and then continuously revised them as he grew older and wiser.

The second learning is this: We need to be in earnest prayer that the directions found in age-less wisdom are a consistent part of our life journey. We need daily prayer for less concern with success and more commitment to faithfulness. We need to earnestly ask God for less concern with schedule and more concern for others. We need the Spirit's presence to help us gravitate away from self-centeredness and toward works of compassion. We need to claim God's passion for justice and the foolishness of all forms of greed. We need to be responsible adults with a childlike way of seeing.

I want to be a grandpa who improves with age. I want to nurture that inner being of my life so that what flows from me is a witness to life's most cherished values. I shall wear my sweatshirt on many occasions yet to come with prayer for wisdom and for the ability to pass such wisdom on to my precious grandchildren. May God grant us all the grace to improve with age.

# Special Delivery

For many years, my summer garden seed order was placed by mail within days of the catalog delivery, usually in the week between Christmas and New Year's. There was something about doing it right away that made the process a harbinger of spring in my life.

About the second week of January, our doorbell would ring. It was the postal delivery person on his rounds. For many years, it was the same individual. Each year, he had the same incredulous, knowing smile on his face when I came to the door. And each year, he handed me the small box with the seed company logo stamped all over it as he spoke the same words: "Here's your garden, Reverend!"

Something inside of me could not wait to inspect the order. I would carefully open the box within minutes. Inside were about two dozen packets of seeds, some advertisements for gardening products, and an extra pre-addressed mailing form for a second order in case I had forgotten anything. Occasionally, there was a new hybrid strain of seed which I was invited to try in the coming season.

Every year, I would study the seed packets carefully. I would review how many weeks before the last frost were required so that seeds could be planted indoors. For a few hardy types, the seeds could actually be started in mid-February. I could scarcely wait.

The regular delivery and the subsequent inner excitement during those years became a symbol of hope in my life. The planting season would come again. Growing season would return. God had promised, and I could count on it.

The very first sermon I preached after I made my decision to enter the ministry was based on I Peter 3:15. I am quite sure that the actual sermon was poor at best, but the text stands as a key one for my life, and for yours: "Always be ready to give account for the hope that is in you."

"Hope" was my first word in preaching many years ago. If I ever preach a "last" sermon, it will be a message on the sure and certain hope in the Good News of Jesus Christ.

Vegetable seeds, ordered in late December and delivered in mid-January, affirm the essential hope that shall never disappoint us.

# Choosing the Top Bunk

> *"But as for that in the good soil, these are the ones who, when they hear the word, hold it fast in an honest and good heart, and bear fruit with patient endurance."*
> *(Luke 8:15)*

When Matthew and Andrew were ages three and one, they began occupying the same bedroom in their home. It seemed prudent to their parents that this new arrangement be made at the first of the new year. Appropriately, they purchased bunk beds.

When he first saw the beds in place, Matthew immediately announced that he would select the top bunk. As the oldest, he felt the prerogative to be his. On the first night of the new adventure, he crawled onto the top, and began to prepare the blankets for sleep. For the first time he looked down. From this fresh and unexpected perspective, he quickly decided that perhaps, just perhaps, this was not such a good idea after all. He immediately returned to ground-level security.

When I talked to him by phone a few days later, I said, "Matthew, are you sleeping in the top bunk now?"

The reply came immediately and firmly, "Later, Poppa, later."

Top-level spiritual maturity cannot be presumed for us by others. It is a matter of growth, and comes in God's own time for each of us. We cannot be forced to step out upon a new adventure or make a radical new leap of faith before we are ready. The challenge is there; the goal is evident; God's claims are real; but the timing is commensurate with each person's inner journey.

God is patient with us. All God really asks is that we set our sights appropriately, and that we be willing to grow. Like Matthew, we will take the next step. But "Later, Poppa, later!" It will come when God has built a preparedness within us.

Strive for "top bunk" spirituality in your faith journey. Courageous discipleship will prod you toward new vitality and spiritual discipline in the days ahead. Count on it. It is God's way among Christ's people.

# Back-ordered

Let us hold fast to the confession of our hope without wavering, . . . not neglecting to meet together, as is the habit of some. (Hebrews 10:23, 25)

One year, my mail-order garden arrived right on schedule on a cold, wintry day. Typically, I needed to sort through a lot of packing materials in the box before getting to the actual seed packets. All seemed to be in good order.

Then I spotted the computer-generated packing slip in the bottom of the box. In twenty-five years or more of ordering seeds, I had never seen one quite like it.

I read the slip carefully. Everything I had ordered was included—with two exceptions. Two items would be shipped later. And what were these two items? I could scarcely believe my eyes: beans and tomatoes! They didn't have the beans and tomatoes in stock!

Now I ask you: can you imagine running out of beans and tomatoes in a garden seed supply company? Surely there must be some mistake. Even those who have only a few square feet of home garden grow beans and tomatoes. A company might be out of stock of some exotic okra seed, or a rare hot pepper, or special hybrid cantaloupe, but not the basic staples of garden produce.

But there the words were, clearly printed. *Back-ordered: beans and tomatoes. Will be shipped as soon as available.*

Sometimes, the Christian life is like that seed order. We run out of the basic stuff of the journey. We may be actively involved in a whole host of significant ministries and activities, but our worship and prayer life are "back-ordered." We try to grow life's garden without the essentials.

Sometimes, the encroachment of the world so impinges upon our lives that we run out of the staples—the beans and tomatoes—which keep life meaningful and on track. We have a full complement of life's goods, but we do not have hold of those things which really matter.

Sometimes we just forget. In the seemingly ordered chaos of our daily lives, we forget to worship weekly. We forget to pray. We get out of the habit. Sometimes, for weeks at a time! Suddenly, we are back-ordered, and the garden of life seems empty.

Inventory your spiritual catalog. Check the seeds of your life's garden. Are some essential elements missing? Are staples absent from your varied list?

No backyard garden should be without beans and tomatoes. No thriving, resilient Christian life is adequate without worship and prayer.

# Unafraid

*Surely God is my salvation; I will trust, and will not be afraid, for the LORD GOD is my strength and my might; he has become my salvation. (Isaiah 12:2)*

This was a momentous occasion. Grandma and I were to take Matthew to his very first movie. He had seen a few films on television and on video, but not yet at the theater. *Bambi* had just arrived for its classic reissue in the theaters. The timing was ideal. Delighted grandparents and grandson would go.

Matthew was an eager three-year-old. The sense of adventure was written on his face and in his body language. He burned a lot of energy in sheer anticipation.

We took our seats about five minutes before the picture began. Matthew declined to sit on our laps but preferred to sit between us, raised up a bit by sitting with his legs folded under him. The movie began. He excitedly called out the names of Thumper and Petunia and the Wise Old Owl as they appeared in the story. He was fully familiar with these wonderful characters.

Soon, Bambi was born. The plot began to unfold. I glanced over and saw that Matthew was in rapt attention. Gradually, he changed positions so as to sit in the seat in a more normal fashion. I asked if he could see, and was assured that he could. He was in awe of it all, and was intensely involved in the movie—or so I thought.

Then came the devastating and terrifying fire in the forest. (I had forgotten the drama of that part of the movie.) The animals raced through the forest looking for protection. The fire raged furiously. Various animals cried out frantically to one another. I glanced over at Matthew to be sure he was OK. He was sound asleep.

Only a small child could be secure enough to sleep through the forest fire in *Bambi*. No fear! No threat! No loss of trust toward life! Just: "I'm tired from all the excitement and anticipation of this. I think I'll sleep now!" Beautiful! No wonder Jesus lifted up the simple trust of children for us to model.

God's Providence is everywhere. Ultimately, we have nothing to fear. The world is not always a gentle place, but God can be trusted to be present absolutely. Isaiah spoke to the matter centuries ago. Paul may have said it best when he said that nothing in all creation can separate us from the love of God in Christ Jesus our Lord. (Romans 8:38-39.)

Matthew will undoubtedly see *Bambi* innumerable times in his young life. But no time will be as special—or as instructive to his grandparents—as the first time!

# Clay Pots

*We have this treasure in clay jars, so that it may be made clear that this extraordinary power belongs to God and does not come from us. (II Corinthians 4:7)*

During the early years of my gardening hobby, I acquired a large number of clay pots. They were of the familiar variety, reddish brown in color with a small hole in the bottom. Some were purchased in garden stores. Some were given to me by "retired" gardener friends. Some were acquired inexpensively at garage sales. Some came with purchased plants. And some just seemed to appear.

However, they did not last. They cracked easily. Over the years, they would crumble apart in my hands. Some would even disintegrate when they fell to the soft, newly cultivated soil of the garden. Gradually, they became too expensive to replace. And those which were purchased seemed increasingly fragile.

The planting pots of the next generation were often manufactured from pressed peat, a material that could be planted directly into the soil. A few of these single-use pots were in trays out of which the seedlings could be individually lifted for planting. Occasionally, I surrendered to plastic pots as well. Ecological concerns quickly ended that development.

Somewhere along the way, while holding one of the original species of clay pots in my hands, a verse of Paul from his letter to the Corinthian

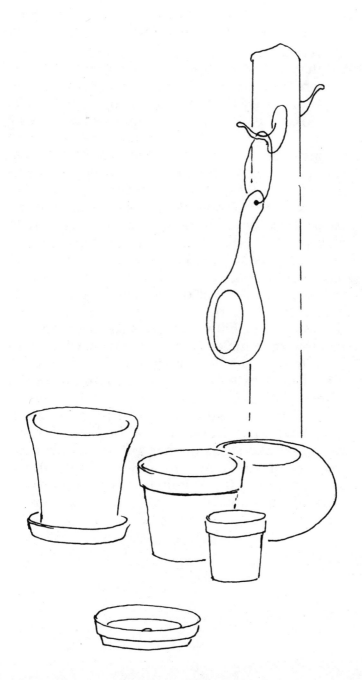

church came to mind. He reminded them (and us) that we are like common clay pots.

Were my garden pots those which Paul had in mind? Paul was probably referring to water jars or cooking pots. But the character of the vessel itself has remained fundamentally the same through the centuries. Paul was saying, "We are common. We are breakable. We do not last indefinitely."

However, Paul does not leave us "in the dust." He goes on to say more: "We have . . . treasure in clay jars." We have immortal tidings in these mortal hands of ours. We carry a treasure within our mortal being.

The treasure is variously identified as eternal life, or as a faith by which to live. The power of this treasure is that which gives us the capacity to be more than merely human in our reach toward the Life to which Jesus invites us. The power is a gift of God extended through common mortal beings.

We have a treasure, a hope, a promise, a gift which we carry in our mortal bodies. May we recognize the signs of that gift anew. May the treasure of abundant life come upon us, transform us, and endure within us as vessels of God's purpose in creation.

# Broccoli with Cheese

> *Christ Jesus . . . emptied himself, taking the form of a
> slave, being born in human likeness. . . . God also
> highly exalted him and gave him the name that is above
> every name, so that at the name of Jesus every knee
> should bend. (Philippians 2:5-10)*

One early April Saturday, Matthew telephoned his instructions for the spring planting of the coming season's garden. For his younger brother, he ordered corn on the cob and tomatoes. For himself, the order was broccoli with cheese!

Broccoli with cheese! Has the enterprising seed growing industry produced a new hybrid variety? Did I miss something in the seed catalogs this year?

Like Matthew, I do enjoy broccoli—and grow lots of it each summer. About two dozen seedlings are either readied on a sunny window sill or (as in more recent years) purchased from a local grower. This somewhat "new" vegetable in the western world is quite possibly the most singularly nutritious crop one can grow.

Broccoli with cheese simply accentuates what is already the best. The sensation of melted sharp cheddar over the freshly steamed spears of nutritional wonder from the garden is virtually incomparable.

Likewise, Easter accentuates what is already the best news ever. We are initially fed and nourished by the quality of life and love in Jesus' earthly ministry. We are given new insights as to what constitutes the highest and best that the human experience can ever know. We are called to an extraordinary discipleship. We are loved and forgiven by an amazing act of grace on that "hill far away."

Easter becomes the grandest climax to the already great good news. God entered this life in earthly form. God also raised Jesus to give us an incredible hope and confidence. Easter is, therefore, the indispensable garnish upon the best that life offers. It is God's glorious complement to a disciple's life journey.

How often truth is best seen in simple images, and in the innocent comments of children.

I promised Matthew lots of broccoli during that particular growing season. And grandma promised to cook it carefully, preserving the vitamin-rich content and adding plenty of cheese. Best of all, in our home and extended family, the Easter celebration that year had a new image through which to attempt an understanding of the greatest wonder of God's love on behalf of us all.

# Iced Crocus

*We are afflicted in every way, but not crushed; . . .
struck down, but not destroyed. (II Corinthians 4:8-9)*

Traditionally, the tiny crocus is the first flower in our geographical area to emerge as winter moves into spring. Late one winter, warmth in the air sent a signal to the germ of life in our crocus bulbs. It was time for them to begin their pilgrimage toward the sun. A few green shoots appeared.

Suddenly, a fierce remnant of winter hit our area with snow and bitter cold. One would have thought the crocuses could not withstand five-degree temperatures and wind blasts of severe magnitude. Ice formed around the shoots, and the cold remained for nearly ten days.

But the crocus is durable and resilient. When the weeks of warmer weather inevitably prevailed, the bright blooms of yellow, violet, and blue had appeared as the first colorful harbingers of spring.

God has given the human spirit a remarkable durability and resiliency in our earthly journey. There is a spark within us that is clearly the handiwork of the Creator. By faith, the spark glows, grows, and burns brightly. We are touched by grace and thereby withstand the coldest wintry-like blasts of doubt and disaster. Paul writes persuasively to the Corinthian church of the remarkable resiliency of the Christian life.

The season of early spring frequently parallels the observance of Holy Week for the Christian. Sometimes, Holy Week and Easter come very early on the calendar. Occasionally, the sacred season comes at the last week of March, just when the crocus blooms are at their fullest.

The events and message of Holy Week are encouragement for our lives. They bring a sure and certain hope in the midst of bleak winters of the spirit. The message is one of the eternal promises which will not be broken.

The delicate durability of the lowly crocus is a wonder to behold. This little flower is surely a symbol of the tenacity of faith, and of the blossom of hope. May the spring crocus blooms in our lives have a special measure of beauty and significance for our steadfast journey.

# From Brown to Green

*The wilderness and the dry land shall be glad, the desert shall rejoice and blossom. (Isaiah 35:1)*

Duringg April and May, my vegetable garden is a basic brown. The soil may be rich in dormant nutrients, but it is still brown. There are few significant signs of life. Even the early onset of weeds and the germination of a few vegetable seeds does not change the fundamental appearance.

By mid-summer, however, it is a lush, vital green. Huge cauliflower leaves spread wide in anticipation of the formation of tasty white curds. Corn stands six or seven feet tall, brimming with ears ready for boiling water on the kitchen stove. Broad, deep green leaves hide the wonder of succulent acorn squash. Carrot ferns stand as sentinels to the wondrous taproots below ground. The thick foliage of eggplant and pepper almost hide the weighty suspended fruits beneath. Lush red tomatoes hang on think green vines. And at least two varieties of beans hang heavy, ready for harvest. The brown has become an explosion of green in the miracle of growing things.

Christianity rose out of a desert culture. Our faith roots have origins in the hot, dry, brown desert sands: Abraham, Isaac, Jacob, Rachel, Ruth, Isaiah, Moses, John, Jesus, and Paul. The noteworthy issue is this: each of these forebears of our Faith passionately believed that the desert of our lives was soil for blossoming faith-filled

living. They knew the tranforming power of God's goodness on their behalf. They lived that hope, and they proclaimed it.

As Christian disciples on today's faith journey, we are a community of people in the legacy of desert teachings that go back more than four thousand years. Barren lives can be transformed into fruitful living. Brown can turn to green. Such is the wisdom and wonder of Faith. No matter how arid, how barren, how dusty our lives, the Grace of God can transform the brown desert into green pastures.

"The desert shall rejoice," shouted Isaiah. Such is the hope and promise of our lives. Without exception! God can turn any brown into green. Rejoice in that expectation.

# Simultaneous Stretching

A clematis plant supported by an aluminum trellis now grows in a partially shaded area in our yard. Seasonally, the clematis produces large numbers of beautifully delicate flowers.

About two weeks after the original planting, a strange phenomenon began to appear in the plant's growth pattern. Two new shoots were moving evenly upward. At the end of each shoot were three tiny prongs, each with a budding leaf at the end. The two shoots seemed to resemble two praying hands. The hands were simultaneously stretching upward toward the light *and* also stretching toward the trellis, trying to grasp the various sections for growth support.

What a marvelous parable from nature. We, too, stretch authentically in two directions at the same time. On the one hand, we stretch toward God, toward the Light, toward the Source of life's energy and meaning. On the other hand, we reach out to grasp life firmly, holding on, embracing the "here and now" of our existence.

The clematis helps us appreciate the meaning of prayer as well. Prayer is reaching toward God. The very nature of prayer challenges us to take hold of life with all the promise that God gives it.

These observed growth patterns remind us of the dual dimension of true discipleship. We are to reach toward God in acts of worship and devotion. And we are to be in the world in acts of compassion and justice. Our lives in Christ are complete only when we seek a spiritual base as well as become a caring presence among God's children.

Reach up! Stretch mightily toward that One in Whom we live and move and have our being. And—at the same time—reach out. Reach out to enfold the world, this planet, which is God's gift. Stretch both ways, to enjoy the holistic dimension of life abundant. And give God thanks for an intricate little flower that reminds us of our most appropriate stance before God.

# Leaning on the Everlasting Arms

> "Blessed are the poor in spirit, for theirs is the kingdom of heaven." (Matthew 5:3)

Typical of many toddlers, Casey had a mind of her own. She was bright, alert, and never missed a beat with regard to what was going on. She did not formulate many words, but she understood our adult conversations very well. She responded to invitations or instructions with clear understanding and with instant opinions.

The decision was made to go swimming. Her two older brothers made ready with considerable exuberance. They had recently become fairly comfortable in the water. Casey would follow their lead. She was not to be left behind.

When we arrived at the pool, the boys headed straight for the water. Casey looked at them, then at us, and instantly determined what her position would be for the duration: in her mother's arms, tightly. The water frightened her. She would go in, but only if held securely by the one in whom she had utmost confidence. No one else would suffice.

Learning our limits is a lesson that many of us must re-learn in adult life. At some point, we rediscover our humanity, our mortality, and our vulnerability. And we know that we need to be held in the arms of our heavenly Father. If we are to make it through this pilgrimage of life victoriously, we need to know the One upon Whom to lean.

Many years ago, a Bible scholar taught me that this was precisely the meaning of the first Beatitude of Jesus. He also suggested that Jesus intended the first Beatitude to be the most important lesson we must learn. "Blessed are the poor in spirit" literally means "blessed are those who know that they need God." Blessed are those who know that in order to be even moderately adequate to the living of these days, we must lean into the everlasting arms.

How easy to be reminded of this by a self-aware and beautiful granddaughter. How easily we become so sure and self-contained, assuming we can make it on our own. How crucial that we re-learn one of Jesus' most important spiritual teachings.

I know the message with escalating power and veracity in my own journey, especially as I grow older. May you know it as well, with all the promise which the Master intended.

# Kentucky Wonder

> *Philip found Nathanael and said to him, "We have found him about whom Moses in the law and also the prophets wrote, Jesus son of Joseph from Nazareth. . . . Come and see." (John 1:45-46)*

One of the greatest taste sensations from the home garden is freshly picked Kentucky Wonder pole beans. I remember savoring them as a child from my father's garden. And I now plant a few in my own garden patch each year.

In one recent summer, we had an incredibly difficult growing season in our area. Because of some extended weeks of drought, the rabbits and birds came after fresh bean sprouts not simply for food, but also for moisture. Only after three plantings and a careful fencing did my small crop of pole beans finally get established.

Early one July afternoon, I noticed some of the bean vines were headed off into emptiness. Instead of climbing the carefully placed poles, they were reaching out for some nonexistent support in the opposite direction. Carefully, and gently, I pulled the vine leaders from each misdirected plant toward the three poles, which formed a kind of tripod in the ground. I loosely wound each leader around one of the poles and hoped for the best.

Within hours, success was apparent. Each bean plant leader had quickly and tightly wrapped itself around the pole as though in reunion with a long-lost lover or family member. It was a marvelous phenomenon of nature to behold. Even after such a short time span, these plant leaders could not have been removed or changed from their new allegiance without seriously damaging the plant. They clutched the poles tenaciously.

How many persons around us are reaching out into emptiness these days, yearning for something solid upon which to cling? Do you know someone so disillusioned with the emptiness of life that he or she is reaching for something more substantial, enduring, or stable? Perhaps a neighbor? A family member? A friend? A co-worker?

Scores of people await only the caring, gentle assistance of a Christian friend to lead them to the firmly promised support of faith. Their longing may not be quite as apparent as those of my pole beans, but it is present and very intense. If such persons are simply encouraged, nudged, assisted, or invited in the direction of the authentic support of life, they will attach themselves and find their true home in due course.

The simplest, most loving invitation we can bring is the one Philip offered to Nathanael centuries ago: "Come and see."

# Fast Food Convenience

> *They heard the sound of the LORD God walking in the garden at the time of the evening breeze. (Genesis 3:8)*

Ours is the life-style of the convenience store and the fast food restaurant. Our quickened pace and full schedules have created an industry that is thriving. Convenience stores are on every corner. And the hand-held breakfast is the fastest growing "eat out" meal in America.

Perhaps this is part of the reason I love my garden so much. A garden may not save much money. And garden vegetables aren't really that much more nutritious than fresh vegetables purchased at the supermarket. Gardening takes time. Preparing the foods even from a small harvest requires an extra half hour or so. But the benefits quickly multiply.

I thought of this as I picked some fresh green bush beans from my backyard plot one July day. Picking beans is slow, often back-aching work. After they are picked, they must be snapped and washed and cooked and prepared for the table. Those beans which are not eaten in a few hours require further attention for freezing.

Beans don't wait until it's convenient for you to harvest them. When they are ready, they are ready. Beans are not prepared for the table in "thirty minutes or less." It is a slow, precious, time-consuming process. Garden beans don't care if your schedule is full, or if you worked all day and arrived home tired at 6:30 P.M. Garden beans don't care if you only have 45 minutes between getting home from work and an evening appointment.

A lesson, then, from the lowly green bean. When life is too busy for a bit of bean harvesting in the summer, it is probably too busy. When life has no time to savor the harvest, the snapping, and the slow cooking of green beans (with a bit of bacon thrown in), then time is probably too full of too many things. When there is no time to think and reflect while perched on a makeshift stool above a beautiful, lush, heavy-laden row of green bush beans once in a while, then time needs to be re-evaluated.

Such reflections may represent a minority opinion in this day and age. But I will vastly prefer a mess of beans, an hour or two from the garden, over fast food and convenience food any time.

Remember that life began in a garden. It is no trivial observation that God walked in the garden in the cool of the evening. May we not get too far away from that part of our sacred Story.

# Safari Adventure

*For this I toil and struggle with all the energy that he powerfully inspires within me. (Colossians 1:29)*

Matthew was twenty months old. We thought it was a good time for him to visit the African Lion Safari near our vacation cottage. It would be a trip in which everyone would remain in the car. And it was one of those special outings alone with Grandma and Grandpa. Armed with a few dollars and some discount coupons, we drove out toward the "jungle" for the Safari adventure.

As we paid at the gate, we purchased the requisite small bag for feeding the animals. Matthew could already see the various animals on the horizon as we began the slow drive through the park. He was instantly thrilled. While he was not yet offering many intelligible words, he shrieked and laughed as the giraffe tried to stick his head in the window for food, or as the old elk nudged the side of our car. He fed the animals, savored each creature that came along, and bounced with tireless energy and emotion on his grandmother's lap as we slowly circled the park.

When we had completed our twenty-minute driving tour, we learned that we could make a second lap if desired. Knowing that Matthew had thoroughly enjoyed the first trip, we bought another bag of food, drove through the gate, and began the circle again.

Alas, Matthew's energy was spent. He had so thoroughly depleted his emotional energy and ecstasies on the first trip that he had nothing left for Round Two. Within moments, he was sound asleep.

Grandma and Grandpa finished the second tour with Matthew blissfully in the land of dreams.

Would that we all could savor each new adventure of the Christian journey with as much enthusiasm and wonder as Matthew did that first trip through the Safari Park. Would that we could expend ourselves and our energies to such an extent. God calls us to put all that we have and are into each new day of the pilgrimage of this life. And when it is over, we sleep with the peace of knowing that we have given our best, and lived the days of our journey to the fullest extent possible. We rest securely in the arms of the Eternal.

# Bare Necessities

*"Therefore I tell you, do not worry about . . . your body, what you will wear. Is not life . . . more than clothing? . . . But strive first for the kingdom of God and his righteousness." (Matthew 6:25, 33)*

Two-year-old Casey does not particularly care for wearing clothes. She finds them cumbersome and confining. Her happiest part of the day is bath time when she can run around the house for a while, unrestricted by clothes.

It is difficult to keep her dressed. Shoes and socks are always missing, strewn in various, not necessarily contiguous locations. Dresses are a particular problem. When very young, Casey could not crawl easily when in a dress, and she struggled while attempting to nagivate steps or trying to stand.

Of course, those times when it is most appropriate for her to be in a pretty dress are also occasions when she is not likely to be distracted by play. Recently she tried to disrobe during our son's wedding. She is unmindful of the surroundings and not yet aware of social graces. She wants to be rid of the offending garments, and it does not matter if she is in a restaurant, in church, in the yard at play, or enveloped within the privacy and security of home.

Jesus reminded us that we should be concerned with how we clothe our *inner* selves. Bodily garb is not really significant. We must not be concerned with appearance, styles, or labels. Rather, we should concentrate on the work of God's Kingdom and those garments which suit God's people: compassion, kindness, humility, meekness, patience, forbearance, forgiveness and love (Colossians 3:12ff.).

As Casey matures, she will acquire modesty and better understand social conventions. As she has grown in stature, moving around in a dress has become easier. Already, she wants a voice in choosing her outfit for the day.

Casey still needs help in getting dressed. Assuredly, as she grows in years, she will need continued help in clothing her spirit.

We all need help in clothing our spirit. May we strive to wear God's wardrobe for the inner being without feeling constrained or hampered as we move about in the world in which we live. May we "put on" the garments of discipleship and follow the Master Teacher. This is clothing we wear with a marked difference in our Christian walk.

# The Big Puddle

Matthew loves the water. From a very early age he relished any opportunity to play on a warm day in a wading pool or any standing water provided by Mother Nature. As he has grown, so has the size of the body of water preferred for swimming.

In the late spring of his second year, Matthew had his first trip to the ocean. We arrived at our vacation residence along the ocean shore, and he immediately began to explore the rooms in the big beach house. Before long, he was standing out on the deck, looking in wide-eyed wonder at the ocean just fifty or sixty feet away. He looked at his mother, and with a face full of eager anticipation, he exclaimed, "Wow! Big puddle!"

The ocean is a big puddle indeed. It is such in the eyes of God, and in the eyes of a small child. Perspective is important. Sometimes it is significant to look at life and the world as God must see them. Children help us do that.

What often seems to us to be so very large and overwhelming is, to God, very minute. When we learn to depend upon God, and learn to see our problems in the fullest possible context, they become far more manageable. Perhaps this is what Jesus most wanted his disciples to learn

when caught in a storm on the Sea of Galilee centuries ago.

The ocean of life is immense. Any crisis can take on an endless expanse with no sight of the farther shore. The stormy tumult of ocean waves can be overwhelming at times. But to see that seemingly endless expanse through God's eyes, and to lean upon God—as we are freely invited to do—is to reduce it to the more manageable proportions of a puddle.

# A Priceless Invitation

> *And Jesus said to them, "Follow me and I will make you fish for people." And immediately they left their nets and followed him. (Mark 1:17-18)*

It was a hot summer day, and all three grandchildren were visiting for a week. The two boys were splashing in a wading pool set up by Grandma in the backyard. The youngest, newborn Casey, was napping nearby. I was upstairs in my study putting the finishing touches on a sermon.

Suddenly, there was a small, insistent voice at the bottom of the stairs: "Poppa! [followed by mixed gibberish, and then] bubba hoop!" It was three-year-old Andrew calling me for something.

"What do you want, Andrew?"

Again: "[mixed gibberish] bubba hoop."

Repeatedly, I tried to ascertain what he was saying. I knew it was a request of some kind, but I could not interpret. Finally, I summoned the linguistic specialists from other parts of the house: Grandma, Mother, and older brother. What is he saying? Once again, Andrew carefully made his request—still ending with the curious words, "bubba hoop."

With a chorus of giggles and wide smiles, the definitive interpretation came. "He wants you to get into your bathing suit and join him in the wading pool!" The adults shared a great laugh. Andrew gave an audible sigh of satisfaction. And, recognizing the intensity of his request to me, I made ready to join him immediately. I met him and Matthew at the small wading pool, stepped in, and immediately took up most of the available space! But Andrew was pleased. His mission had been accomplished.

I have often puzzled over the response of the first disciples to Jesus' call. Did they look at each other as though to say, "What is He asking?" Did they try to find help in discerning what this itinerant preacher from Nazareth was asking of them?

And what about the first-century Roman world? Many of them never did really understand what excited the Christian believers. Nor did they understand the joy, the inexorable faith, and the vision of hope which dominated the spirit of the first disciples.

Understanding and assimilating the call to "follow Him" takes a while at times. Knowing what it means to pursue the "way of truth and life" requires a very close listening process.

The fullest maturing in our understanding frequently takes the help of others who can assist us in clarifying the mystery of the Word in the words. God may use any number of helpers to connect us with the essential meaning of life. But when we finally hear, we are to respond with enthusiasm and vigor. God will not disappoint us.

# The Home Run

. . . and a little child shall lead them. (Isaiah 11:6)

We had arrived just in time to see Matthew's T-Ball game. Complete with big-league baseball titles (the Orioles), custom-made jerseys (black and orange), official caps and shoes (complete with real rubber cleats on the shoes), coaches (a group of willing fathers), and the official athletes' drink (Gatorade) waiting to be served, the team took the field to play the first inning.

T-ball is a bit different from regular baseball. A pitcher simulates a pitch from the mound, and the batter then tries to hit a soft baseball-sized ball off a stationary "T." The inning is over when every batter has had one "at bat." They only play four innings. And no one keeps score! But it is appropriate to the age and experience of five-year-olds.

I watched as the coaches showed these young boys how to hold a bat, how to run the bases, how to lead off the base (and which direction to run!), and when to keep moving. Heretofore, I guess I assumed all such information came instinctively to any boy. Clearly, this is not always the case.

Occasionally, when one of the team members did not show up, three-year-old Andrew was allowed to play ball. Much of the time, he watched intently from the sidelines. Today, he was allowed to play.

He stepped to the plate, swung the bat with considerable precision and force, and sent a ball beyond second base into the outfield. Immediately, he knew exactly what to do. He ran the bases with exactness while his five-year-old "teammates" cheered. Those on the other team chased, threw, and dropped the ball in the outfield. He rounded third base, and made a humorous but effective slide into home plate. It was a home run.

Andrew had been watching and listening. He had heard the repeated instructions of the coaches to each boy. He had not missed any of the important advice. He ran the bases in joyful obedience.

Is this something like what the prophet Isaiah meant when he said, ". . . and a little child shall lead them"? The instructions of the Master for discipleship are relatively simple. When we listen to those instructions with even a small modicum of attentiveness, we are able to run the race of life in joyful obedience.

The word is given in love and graciousness such as a child understands. Even initial obedience requires both determination and trust. They are words that may not be quickly understood by all persons. But they are the words of Life that lead us Home.

# Forehead

> "Let your light shine before others, so that they may see your good works and give glory to your Father in heaven." (Matthew 5:16)

My wife phoned from our daughter's home in Virginia. She had gone to spend two days with our grandsons while their mother attended an out-of-town educational event. She was laughing so hard she could barely tell me the story.

The three of them had been out somewhere in the community. Apparently, two-year-old Andrew had spotted someone whom he thought looked like me. "Look, Ernie," he called to his grandmother, "there's Poppa."

"He looks a bit like Poppa," answered my wife, "but Poppa could not come with me this time."

Whereupon, Matthew chimed in to correct his younger brother. "That's not Poppa, Andrew. Poppa has a forehead in the back of his head that's round!"

Matthew, of course, was referring to a rather distinguishing mark which clearly indicates the absence of hair on the back of my head!

Each of us has his or her special distinguishing marks! Are there also distinguishing signs of our being Christian in the world? So often we are known to be Christian by that which we say or do, or by the way we live in the world, or by our attitudes. Jesus seems to call us to this awareness.

We are to live according to the highest and best that we know. We are to address the world with love, with generosity, and with a clear understanding of grace. We are to evidence some holiness in our lives—even when such holiness may seem to be outdated. We are to bear witness in the world through disciplined acts of worship, devotion, compassion, and justice.

Matthew's comment reminds me of our covenant to live with some clearly distinguishing marks in this wondrous journey. Such living is to be an act of praise to God. If the "mark" (such as a round forehead in the back!) is amusing to others, we simply smile and offer the best that God has shown in determination and discipleship.

One never knows what dialogue between two preschool brothers might offer. On this occasion, I think they may have been on to something.

# A Working Definition

*He also said, "The kingdom of God is as if someone would scatter seed on the ground . . . and the seed would sprout and grow, he does not know how."*
(Mark 4:26-27)

Someone gave me a gardener's T-shirt for my birthday. Printed on the shirt is the following definition:

> gar*den*ing, 1. n. the art of killing weeds and bugs to grow flowers and crops for animals and birds to eat.

I like it. And any vintage gardener knows the truth of that definition. One sometimes wonders why laboring in soil is expended in the first place.

Jesus' disciples invariably knew the same feeling at many points. They were no more immune to frustration and discouragement than we are. They sat with Jesus and asked the hard questions: "Lord, why isn't the crop better? Why do the tangible results seem so limited? Is all this work going to bear any significant fruit at all? Are any lives really changed?"

And Jesus told them a parable (Mark 4:26-27). "Listen," He said. "You are simply called to plant the seed and then do a reasonable amount of caring for the garden. God will bring results. The 'results' are not your responsibility. Just plant and care for the garden as best you can. Let God do the rest."

At times, we need those words of encouragement. Just as we need them when Peter Cottontail mows down a fresh row of bean spouts, or Bugsy Beetle decimates the rhubarb leaves, or Amanda Aphid does in the eggplant foliage, or Gargantuan Groundhog decimates the rest. At the feeling level, you want to cry out, "Why bother?"

The same questions can be asked about one's faith journey. But God is good, and utterly faithful. The seed sprouts and grows, we know not how. Transformations take place. New growth emerges in unexpected places. Lives bear fruit in new and exciting ways.

That is precisely why I have never been discouraged about the people of Faith. Jesus gave his disciples an encouraging word from the beginning. That same word is for you and for me.

Live the promise. Keep hoeing and pulling weeds. God's crop is a premium variety, and it will yield fruit. Chances are, you will know both the joy of laboring in the garden for others and some very special results in your own soul.

# Savvy Christians

> *Let love be genuine; hate what is evil, hold fast to what is good; love one another with mutual affection; outdo one another in showing honor. . . . Contribute to the needs of the saints; extend hospitality.*
> *(Romans 12:9, 13)*

I parted company with my large garden tiller early one recent summer day. We had sustained a partnership for more than twelve years, but the tiller was getting too much for me to handle—too heavy to lift and somewhat bulky. (I was a bit humbled when the man who responded to my "for sale" ad was a slightly built man in his eighties!)

However, I did acquire a new machine—a smaller, lighter electric tiller. It seems to work well. It's not as powerful. It won't demolish spent corn stalks like the other one. And it won't break up new soil for expanding a garden. But it gets the job done.

With the change in tiller companies came a new magazine. All owners of this new tiller are automatically enrolled in a periodic journal called *Savvy Gardener*. What a classy name! The previous tiller had brought me twelve years of the quarterly *Gardening News*. Now, however, it's *Savvy Gardener*.

It was necessary for me to review my dictionary listing for "savvy" to be sure I knew the meaning. "Savvy" means "practical know-how," to "comprehend" or "understand." I have become a savvy gardener!

Surely, it is essential today that we establish ourselves as savvy Christians. We need practical know-how so as to bring discipleship into the growing vacuum and disorientation of contemporary life. We need to understand the faith, to comprehend what believing means for living. Apparently, the apostle Paul felt the same way as he wrote to the church in Rome. In a clear and masterful style, he outlined practical issues of discipleship: love the good, hate what is evil, contribute offerings, extend hospitality. His full list is beautiful and extensive (Romans 12:9-21).

We need constantly to be growing practical skills in basic discipleship—worship, devotion, compassion, and justice.

Such savvy skills will not be found outside the nurturing and sustaining community of the Church. You and I need the rigorous commitment to learning in Christian education for ourselves and our families. We need the discipline of daily encounter with Scripture, the practice of prayer, the stimulation of dialogue with others, and the constant prodding and uplift of corporate worship.

Build some savvy into your Christian journey these days. Find encouragement in the testimony of many others. Then, do whatever it takes to put yourself in line for growth as disciples of our Lord.

# A Singing Irony

Matthew visited for a week while his parents attended a conference in Dallas. While with us, he attended a Garden Gospel Concert on a beautiful summer evening at our church. That day had already been a long day in his young life, and he quite naturally slept through much of the hour-long music presentation.

However, it was obvious the next day that either he had not been fully asleep or he had assimilated some of the music as he slept! Throughout the day, he could be heard somewhere in our home singing the words of one of the songs the choir had sung the night before: "Soon I will be done with the troubles of the world, the troubles of the world. . . ." He had the words, the tune, and the meter to near perfection.

Once my wife and I got over our amazement at his level of memory and retention, we could not help being amused at the irony of the words sung by a child. Surely, a child of such tender years does not have to contemplate being "set free from the troubles of the world." The more we listened, the more ironic it became. And the more we laughed.

Yet, it is also very true that we do live between the times in God's eternity. We constantly live in the "now" of the earthly journey and in the promise of that perfection which "no eye has seen, nor ear heard, nor the human heart conceived" (I Corinthians 2:9). We do not long to be rid of life; yet we anticipate the grand fulfillment of the promise of God. We do not contrive an escape from the burdens of life, and yet we know that God's ultimate plan is "goodness and mercy . . . forever" (Psalm 23).

Matthew sings on in the innocence of early childhood. And we who have known some of the troubles of the world share the wisdom of an ageless faith. God is with us. God will not fail us or forsake us. God wills a final and ultimate good for all of God's children. Therefore, our hearts are neither troubled nor afraid.

Only the God of Jesus Christ makes that paradox one which is absolutely positive. It is mystery worthy of a quiet prayer of thanksgiving in this very moment.

# To Be a Child Again

*He called a child, whom he put among them, and said, "Truly I tell you, unless you change and become like children, you will never enter the kingdom of heaven."*
*(Matthew 18:2-3)*

One mid-July we loaded our two grandsons in the car and began the long drive to return them to their home. We had enjoyed a delightful week with them, and now headed south with great anticipation and a packed car. The trip, slightly reminiscent of the "Family Circus" cartoon, was a child's delight. And it wasn't bad for the grandparents either.

It began with breakfast at McDonald's. As we headed onto the interstate, children's silly song tapes were requested in the tape player. For lunch, it was a Burger King—but not until we found one that had the requisite playground. (We ate. They nibbled and played!)

Five miles beyond Burger King, Grandma knew of a special school playground. A huge play-gym invited at least a thirty-minute stop. About four o'clock, it was the Dairy Queen stop. Followed by two bathroom stops—at two different times.

During the last leg of the trip, it was more sing-a-long tapes, this time of the Bible song variety. The four of us sang our way "home" with enthusiasm. We arrived about nine hours after leaving home, tired, but upbeat and glad.

It was sheer delight for the children and for the "child" in the two grandparents. I began to see the world afresh through the eyes of a four- and six-year-old. Such a world is filled with wonder and the possibilities of instantaneous opportunity.

Jesus knew the dynamic of a child's spirit well. He called the children to Him, blessed them, and celebrated their capacity for joy. He said that you and I must receive the Kingdom as a child might receive a wonderful surprise—with absolute trust and with wide-eyed enthusiasm.

Thank you, God, for grandchildren. As the bumper sticker says it so well, "If I had known having grandchildren was this much fun, I would have had them first!"

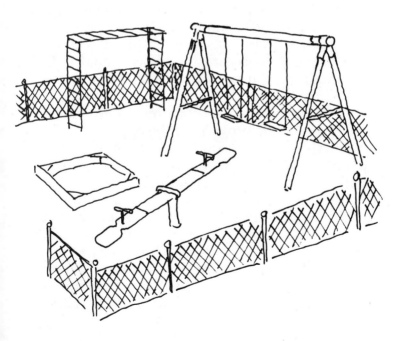

# Declaration of Interdependence

> *Let the nations be glad and sing for joy, for you judge the peoples with equity and guide the nations upon the earth. (Psalm 67:4)*

Grandson Andrew has declared his independence. Such a declaration is a well-documented trait of an almost three-year-old. But sometimes his declaration seems unduly exaggerated.

He insists on opening the freezer door of the refrigerator himself—even though it is quite a struggle. He insists on choosing his own popsicle from the box of assorted colors. He insists on unwrapping the popsicle himself, tussling mightily with both little hands to get the wrapper off the icy treat. He insists on eating it where he wants to eat it—regardless of household guidelines (of course, he gets away with this only at his *grandparents'* house!).

Andrew seems to be oblivious to how dependent he is on the provider of the popsicle.

Each summer season, we mark another Independence Day as a nation. In truth, we are not as independent as we are interdependent.

We certainly celebrate our freedom on this particular holiday. That freedom is precious and still strong. Our liberty should never be taken lightly or cheapened. We rejoice in the Declaration of Independence—a document of hope and promise that gave this nation its birth. And we continue the great traditions of the July Fourth birthday party.

But our contemporary world is surely interdependent—and moving in that direction with accelerating speed. We are a world of interconnected peoples. All of God's children on this planet are tied together in more ways than we know. We belong to one another in a host of ways, and rely upon a rapidly growing number of nations of our world.

Andrew's independent streak is fun to watch. It is at times frustrating for both child and parent. But I am thankful for his sake (and my own) for our great freedom in an interdependent world.

May those who are becoming disciples of our Lord become increasingly aware of the God who draws all people together, Who bids us love and support one another, and who consistently calls us *from* selfishness *toward* a deep connection and interdependence with one another.

In CONGRESS, July 4, 1776.

The unanimous Declaration of the thirteen united States of America,

# Inaugural Wonder

> *The mystery . . . has been hidden throughout the ages and generations but has now been revealed to his saints. . . . How great among the Gentiles are the riches of the glory of this mystery. (Colossians 1:26-27)*

During the first year of his life, Matthew and his parents lived with us. At three months of age, Matthew began to evidence a rapidly growing sense of wonder. And his wonder inevitably triggered my own in a variety of ways. Perhaps the Spirit of God has an easier time teaching wonder when grandchildren are on the scene.

Matthew sat on my lap regularly during those early months, focusing upon every bright or moving object in sight. Occasionally, our eyes met. Quite naturally, in that special moment, I would reward him with the broadest, most adoring smile that any true grandfather could muster.

On one occasion, he focused upon something very special and new. As we sat quietly together, I glanced down to ascertain the object of his attention and realized he was looking with fascination at the pen and pencil set in my shirt pocket. His eyes lit up, his face glowed, and his arms flailed about in every direction. It was as though he was saying, "What are those marvelous things in your pocket, Grandpa? I want to play with them, and I want to play with them now!"

His rapidly developing brain could not yet send the signals to his hands to reach out and grab the pen or pencil. But that time would come in relatively short order.

What will it take to break open our own sense of wonder in the mechanical, insulated world in which we too often make our cocoon?

As I have gradually learned to read the biblical accounts as an act of meditation, I have experienced awe and reverence on countless occasions. I have begun to see and hear and feel great truths that have eluded my more cursory reading or study of the Scriptures. Occasionally, like a small child, I have tried to reach out and grab hold of the mystery. But it will take more time, more growth, and the gentle companionship of the Holy Spirit.

God is ready to open up new mysteries of truth and power to us as we are willing to exercise our sense of wonder. How much richer is our walk of faith when we allow wonder to walk with us.

# Small-scale Soil Erosion

*Finally, be strong in the Lord and in the strength of his power. Put on the whole armor of God, so that you may be able to stand. (Ephesians 6:10-11)*

The backyard of our home lies reasonably flat. However, in this part of the state, any "flatness" is somewhat relative. And my yard does tip slightly from east to west. Aggravations with my plot of garden soil have been minimal. I take care of the soil, replenish it faithfully each growing season, and cultivate it carefully. Even so, over the years I have had one nagging problem. The soil seems somewhat less abundant at the eastern end, and somewhat more abundant on the west. There is a slight "recession" in the soil line at the east, and a slight "hump" at the west. Every couple of years, I have taken several wheelbarrow loads from west to east, but the problem had not disappeared.

It took some time for me to realize that the cause of this phenomenon is soil erosion. Because there is a slight slope, the topsoil is gradually shifting from east to west.

If the garden were planted with grass or other permanent growing things, such erosion would not take place. But given the cyclical nature of a garden, the shift in the precious topsoil is inevitable. I presume that most of it happens between October and May each year. But I never really "see" it take place.

We must pay attention to what is happening to us in the living of our time. Slowly, quietly, the trappings of a modern world erode some part of the sacred from the precious soil of our souls. The accumulation of gadgets to "make life easier," the proliferation of weekend "getaways," the temptation to deplete our bank accounts for long-term membership payments to health spas, vacation packages, and full-season sports packages, and the saturation of television channels from which to choose erode the sacred and accentuate the secular.

For the most part, the secular is not an evil. Perhaps that is why it is such a potential threat. It creeps slowly over our lives, snatching precious moments once used for reading, time with children, marital dialogue, or even weekend worship.

Unless we make every effort to regain some of that precious topsoil of the spirit, unless we put on the whole armor of God, we may find ourselves depleted and deprived of that which gives this human journey meaning and depth.

Agricultural experts warn us of the dangers of soil erosion in the great crop-raising belts of America. I experience a bit of that danger in my own backyard. But even more important, I experience it in the depths of my own soul. Nothing short of clear recognition of what is happening and intentional energies to redirect our lives will solve the problem.

Secular erosion is powerful. But regular communion with God's Spirit is a suitable deterrent.

# Twice Blessed

*Pray without ceasing, give thanks in all circumstances.*
*(I Thessalonians 5:17-18)*

At twenty months of age, Matthew was rapidly beginning to assimilate adult behavior patterns into his life. Some of these patterns are cause for pride and for deeper reflection.

One learned behavior was grace before meals. As a typical child, he began to eat when food was placed in front of him—whether or not others were served (which they usually were not!). When others were seated, however, he was always willing to pause to extend his jelly- or catsup-covered hands, and participate in a brief (very brief) prayer of thanksgiving.

On one occasion, it became apparent that he had gotten the message all too well. He had his sandwich, and I had mine. Each was cut in half. We prayed before we ate. However, when I had consumed the first half and picked up the second half, he suddenly extended his hands with the words, "Amen? Amen?" Clearly, I was to join hands and pray again before enjoying the other half of my sandwich.

Such simple reminders of gratitude are desperately needed. Is it really any surprise that the Apostle Paul tells us to "be constant in prayer" or to "pray without ceasing"? Do we not learn from a little child the undergirding power of thankful hearts?

Not many weeks after this first incident, Matthew did it again. This time, it was with each piece of home-delivered pizza. "Amen, Grandpa? Amen?" His tomato-and-cheese-sauced hands extended earnestly.

Only a child can remind us of how constantly grateful we need to be. Not just the first half, but each half. Not just the first piece, but every piece.

Constancy of gratitude is essential to discipleship. Grateful human beings know the presence of the Almighty. Someone has said that God has two dwelling places. One is in heaven. The other is in a thankful heart. How true!

# Clapping and Praying

*The mountains and the hills before you shall burst into song, and all the trees of the field shall clap their hands. (Isaiah 55:12)*

One of the gifts I received from my wife at the time of our marriage was a sculptured rendering of two praying hands. Those hands have had a prominent place in our living room for nearly thirty years.

One day, shortly after Matthew had turned two years of age, he came into the living room while I was reading. Suddenly, his face was alive with happiness, and his hands were clapping. It took a few moments for me to grasp what was happening. He had noticed the praying hands, assumed they were clapping, and was trying to show me what he had discovered.

"Those are praying hands, Matthew. You know. Amen. Amen." It was the only way I knew how to identify prayer in his experience.

His response was marvelous and instant. He clapped even more exuberantly while saying, "Amen! Amen! Amen!" For me, it was a moment of childlike grace in the presence of God.

Truly, both clapping and praying are a part of our stance before the Holy. We clap for the gift of life, the joy of human ties, and the promise of grace. We pray for strength to stand, for the wisdom to know, and for the peace within, which God alone provides.

Life among believers is an occasion of clapping and praying in one simultaneous sweep. God's people at worship are allowed, encouraged, and prompted to clap and pray, if not outwardly, then certainly within.

Join in the exuberance of a small child. Join in the gathered assembly of God's people. Join with a spouse or friend or Christian colleague. Clap and pray. Pray and clap. With the thrill of a child and the wisdom of age! Rejoice before God with an overflowing heart, and with many hands, and with one voice.

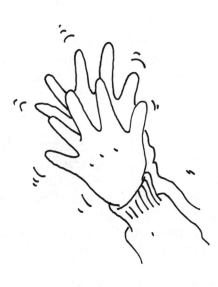

# Time to Do and Be

> But I trust in you, O LORD; I say, "You are my God."
> My times are in your hand. (Psalm 31:14-15)

It was a pleasant afternoon in late September. Such fall days beg one to get some of the outside yard work completed before the onset of cold weather. But there was a dilemma. A very special grandson was in town for a visit. He deserved time and attention. Yet, so did the ragged growth of the hedgerow across the backyard.

The dilemma became acute. Matthew's mother and grandmother went shopping, leaving an energy-laden two-year-old in my supervision and keeping. The quandary? How to get the hedge work done in the two hours of daylight available *and* be a supportive grandfather at the same time. Could one be done without neglecting the other?

The answer turned out to be a positive one. In short order, the hedges were trimmed—interrupted regularly for some delightful squeals of enjoyment during informal soccer practice in the yard. And, to my amazement, there was ample time left over for reading the story of Koko, the gorilla, while lying on the large pillows stacked upon the family room floor.

Undoubtedly, many of us are compulsive about house and yard projects. So little time! So much to do! Yet a very important lesson was learned that September afternoon. In the Providence of God, there is frequently sufficient time to complete what "must" be done, and to have time left for the significant others in our lives. On this particular occasion, the two available hours provided a healthy, marvelous, affirming balance.

God seems to give us sufficient time to "do" and to "be." As one time management teacher put it many years ago, "There is always time to carry out what is important in the eyes of God for a given day." The major impediment is frequently our own inner attitude.

God promises to be with us in what we say, in what we do, and in the smallest decisions and directions of our days.

These thoughts stayed with me a long time after I finished reading the story to Matthew. I cherished those few minutes of closeness and quiet. A prayer of thanksgiving seemed highly appropriate. May God grant us the presence and the wisdom of His Spirit to remember this lesson more frequently in the busyness of our lives.

# Dinosaur Bones

> Such knowledge is too wonderful for me; it is so high
> that I cannot attain it. (Psalm 139:6)

There is something wonderfully enthralling about the dinosaur. Many young children have an avid interest in these strange, prehistoric creatures. Some children even own hand-size replicas of various species that stalked the earth millennia ago. Dinosaur toys come in all shapes and sizes. However, it remains difficult to comprehend a dinosaur's awesome height and breadth with only a model.

Not long ago, I had an opportunity to take Matthew to a museum that has been excavating and doing research on dinosaur bones for decades. The complete skeletal remains of several of these giants have been on display since my own boyhood days.

Matthew was excited about the trip. He showed me his own toy models, and shared a few pictures. We drove to the museum, paid our entrance fee, and headed for the great hall of the dinosaurs. How I wished I had brought a camera to record the first look on Matthew's face as we rounded the corner and entered the room. He stood suddenly still. His eyes grew as big as saucers, and his mouth formed the "oh-h-h" of startled wonder and disbelief. He was definitely not prepared for the size of the display. They exceeded anything his mind had envisioned to that point in time.

We circled the display several times as he stared at these huge remains, and as he asked a few questions. We talked about how they lived and why they probably did not survive. Even as a preschooler, he knew some of the details. Mostly, he circled each skeleton in quiet, awestruck wonder.

Is it not very similar with God's grace? We hear the good news. We read the testimony of Scripture. We learn the testimony of many saints. But do we really have any notion of the majestic scope and wonder of God's creative care for us? Who can truly comprehend the vastness of God's grace and mercy toward our lives? Such knowledge is too wonderful.

For many of us, including young Matthew, we will continue to be startled into a new awareness of God's grace poured out for us. And we may well feel dwarfed by such a revelation. We will stand in reverence and wonder. And that is precisely when the Spirit of God can begin to work God's best and finest in us.

# Putting the Yard to Bed

> *I thank my God every time I remember you, constantly praying with joy in every one of my prayers for all of you. (Philippians 1:3-4)*

**B**its and pieces of several days must be snatched from a busy fall schedule to put the yard to bed around our home. Leaves must be raked and mulched for the garden. Trees and shrubs must be pruned and shaped for the spring. Dead asparagus ferns must be cut down. And a few flowering shrubs must be mulched for the winter to protect delicate root systems from freezing.

It is a time-consuming job, as every homeowner knows so well. Frequently, it produces blisters and sore muscles.

However, the nature of the task is such that it produces some reflection time as well. Unlike putting my grandchildren to bed at night (which takes hours of storytelling and gentle persuading), putting a yard to bed is relatively mindless activity. One does not have to be a strategist of the highest order to rake leaves.

Such reflection time usually brings to mind much for which to be grateful. Paul may have used his trade as a tentmaker to facilitate his own reflection and prayer life. He may have actually used these occasions of sewing and stitching tent fabric to formulate prayers of gratitude for his ministry, for those who demonstrated the Master's way so well, and for abiding friendships and support in his times of greatest difficulty. He writes of how often and faithfully he remembers in thankful prayer all those who have been on this significant journey with him. It is a model worth remembering and emulating.

As the leaves and brush and sagging growth of summer are pulverized in my garden shredder to provide nutrients for good growth for another year, so the thankful thoughts of the Christian journey provide me with energy and incentive to sustain me for whatever lies ahead.

Do you have some relatively mindless task to undertake in the days ahead? Can that task be turned into productive prayers of remembrance and thanksgiving? God's goodness through family, co-workers, and friends is always out there waiting to be received and celebrated in the journey of the faithful.

# Knowing When to Point

*[John, while in prison] sent word by his disciples and said to [Jesus], "Are you the one who is to come, or are we to wait for another?" Jesus answered them, "Go and tell John what you hear and see. . . ."*
*(Matthew 11:2-4)*

The working vocabulary of a two-year-old is supposed to be about fifty words. When Andrew was two, his vocabulary was more limited. His hearing had been temporarily impaired by some tonsil problems and the attendant ear infections. So he communicated by pointing. His pointing was complemented by very pronounced eye contact, facial expressions, and colorful gibberish.

Andrew did not speak many words for yet another reason. His older brother spoke for him. Matthew understood Andrew's intentions very quickly. Before Andrew could begin to form the words, his brother turned to parents or grandparents to explain exactly what request or comment was being made. Andrew would simply nod in affirmation.

But when Matthew was not around, Andrew communicated through pointing. When I would read a book about animals, he would point to the animal and then look at me in obvious delight. It was as though he had named that animal correctly in his thought process, and had done it perfectly.

Someone once said that the most effective form of preaching might be to put one's hand over the mouth and point. Andrew was certainly a partial validation of that observation.

Sometimes there are no words, only gestures and signs. God has given us those gestures through hands and eyes and facial expressions which are powerful communication tools.

This must have been part of the intent of Jesus when the disciples of John came to him. When asked concerning his identity, Jesus pointed to what was happening. "Look around you. Consider what is being done," he suggested. Spoken words are not really necessary here. Rather, a closer personal examination for oneself should suffice to make a dicision.

Andrew's speech began to expand in due course. And the words continue to grow in a steady, flowing stream. But I shall always savor the memories of those months of powerful communication when he simply knew how to point.

May we remember the moment when Jesus quietly but effectively pointed to the events in progress through His ministry, and may we endeavor to point the way for the gospel as God gives us grace.

# The Missing Puzzle Piece

> *"Which one of you, having a hundred sheep and losing one of them, does not leave the ninety-nine in the wilderness and go after the one that is lost until he finds it?"* (Luke 15:4)

Andrew and I were enjoying the piecing together of a new puzzle he had received for his birthday. Slowly, carefully, we found the borders. Then the main sections began to take shape. He would tentatively pick up each piece and turn it a variety of ways to ascertain whether it was a proper fit. I would only help when he let me! And that was not too often.

Gradually, the full picture began to appear on the table. Accordingly, the smiles of delight and satisfaction began to appear on his face.

Suddenly, I heard an "Uh Oh, Poppa!" Something was wrong. His smile had turned to a worried frown. One final piece of his brand new puzzle was missing.

We quickly checked the box. We looked under pieces of newspaper at the other end of the table. We checked the floor. We asked other family members in the house at the time. The more we searched, the more frustrated he became.

I suggested the possibility that the makers of the puzzle had forgotten to include that one piece. Andrew would not buy that argument. He was absolutely certain that the piece could be found *and* that we were not to rest until it was!

After a lengthy search, the missing piece was finally found under the lid of the box on the bench beside us. With great joy and a major sigh of satisfaction, the young puzzle maker inserted the last piece in triumphal glee. Now, and only now, the picture was complete.

Somewhere in the whole process, I began to remember Jesus' words about a lost sheep. Even if one small creature was missing from the large flock, an all-out search would be essential. The loving Creator of the universe would not rest until all were in place. No one was dispensable. No one was unimportant. No one could be left without the intensive search of the Master Shepherd.

Those who have been called into the flock by the compelling voice of this Shepherd are valued beyond all human comprehension. Not one is left alone. No child of the Creator is hidden or misplaced. Otherwise, God utters a divine "Uh Oh!" from the halls of heaven; and a search begins.

On this particular day, a very special little puzzle maker helped me see the intensity of God's passion for each one of us. No wonder Jesus told us to watch for images of God in the eyes and hearts of the children!

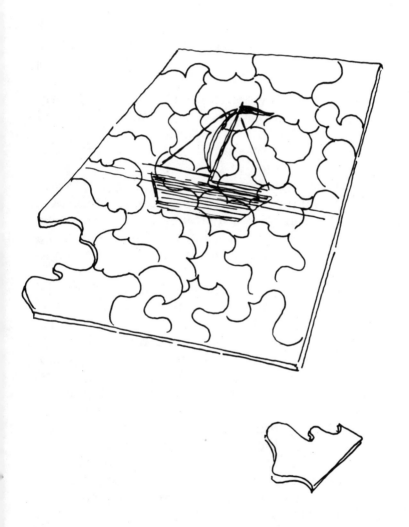

# Useless Growth

> *"Do not store up for yourselves treasures on earth, where moth and rust consume . . . but store up for yourselves treasures in heaven." (Matthew 6:19-20)*

The summer season had produced a fairly good corn crop. The plants had yielded healthy, fully ripened ears for our enjoyment. It was now time to mulch the garden for the winter.

The cornstalks were plowed under, and began the natural process of forming humus for the next growing season. But a strange twist in the cycle of nature resulted. In early October, there was a newly emergent, and presumably healthy stand of corn.

Obviously, it was useless growth. I had plowed under the summer corn crop in early September, including some overripe ears still on the stalks. Then came the warm days and rain of late September. In a quite unusual phenomenon of October weather patterns, we had no killing frosts. Thus, new corn germinated in random patterns everywhere!

Is there anything quite as useless as corn that is knee high on the fourth of October? Perhaps it is appropriate for those who live in Sydney, Australia or Lima, Peru—but not in my backyard!

And that's not all. That year, the October garden produced healthy bean shoots—the same variety that Bugs Bunny fattened himself on in May. More useless growth, of course. And still more! By conservative estimate, about one hundred thousand tomato seedlings literally covered the section of ground where dying parent plants had been plowed under a few weeks earlier. Useless growth!

How much of human energy is spent on useless growth, which has no intrinsic worth or meaning. Our humanity lures us into false growth objectives. We jockey for a preferred position in the right stock or money market fund. We scramble for the highest equity in our home. We diversify our investments and then use the proceeds to grow more investments. We grow in our accumulation of things, and fail to see the uselessness of it all. We never hear the careful, loving, convincing words of the greatest Teacher of all time: "Do not store up for yourselves treasures on earth . . . but store up for yourselves treasures in heaven."

Useful growth, productive growth, refreshing growth are all found in the things of God's kingdom. Such treasures are difficult to quantify in the high-touch, high-tech momentum of our day. But they are the treasures that matter at the deepest level of life, where God and grace and goodness are found.

God is among us to encourage and enable useful growth. Nothing can finally separate us from that glad good news.

# The Legacy of the Three Little Pigs

> *"When your children ask in time to come, 'What do those stones mean to you?' then you shall tell them. . . ."* (Joshua 4:6-7)

My grandchildren love the story of the three little pigs. The story is often a family tradition passed on from grandparent to grandchildren. It is the same story that has warmed and teased the hearts of many children for generations.

By last count, I have purchased at least four different versions of this children's book. I also have my personal rendering of the story which involves action and participation, with appropriate voice inflections and angry pounding on doors.

Not all versions are the same. In one version the wolf eats the pigs. Another version, told from the wolf's perspective, relates how the story is simply a matter of bad press. There is even one book with three small pigs you can hold in your hand while you read the story.

In the version of the story we tell most often, all three pigs survive, and they dance their victory over the wiles and craftiness of the wolf. The wolf gets only slightly scalded and races off to the woods to find healing. The story is read or told with great drama and live action. Matthew and Andrew will offer many of the key lines of the story as it is told, complete with facial expressions and the "y-e-o-o-o-w" of the wolf who falls down the chimney into the hot water.

On one occasion, my wife was telling the story to Matthew, and she gave a woefully frightened voice to the pigs when they feared the wolf might be able to blow down the house of bricks. When she looked up, Matthew had tears streaming down his own cheeks.

How I wish it were possible to tell the stories of faith and faith's adventures even half as well. How I yearn for the time and energy (and creativity) to "tell the old, old Story" in such a way as to commit it to irrevocable memory in the experience of each child for a lifetime.

How important it is to tell "the Story" in such a way as to weep with Peter at his own denial of our Lord, to leap with joy with the lame man healed at the Beautiful Gate of the temple, to go with the women and make the startling discovery of the empty tomb, or to feel the drama of Abraham leaving the familiarity of home at age seventy-five simply because God calls.

We know the classic stories of children's books so well. Children are ready and willing to hear and learn the most wondrous of all stories.

Tell "the Story" to a child this week. Tell it with all the power and drama within you. If necessary, be a bit foolish for Christ and for the sake of the gospel. Dance and sing and laugh and cry. We must be about the telling of our Story.

# Yes! And Amen!

*For in him every one of God's promises is a "Yes." For this reason it is through him that we say the "Amen," to the glory of God. (II Corinthians 1:20)*

Sitting through worship with four-year-old Andrew is an unusual and energy-depleting experience. He is a constant sea of motion. He seems to prefer that hour in the sanctuary to a separate session elsewhere with other children, but one would have to wonder at the wisdom of his own decision-making process on that point.

He talks, asks questions, leafs through the hymnal (upside down), puts his head on the pew and his feet in my lap (followed by the exact reverse), kicks the pew in front of us, crawls under the pew, and asks if it is over about one dozen times!

How could he possibly gain anything from that hour of sanctuary worship exposure?

Yet, he astounded me recently. I had joined the congregation in the singing of "Amazing Grace." Suddenly, I was aware of Andrew singing from the pew where he was still seated. He was right on key, hymnal open and upside down. As I listened more carefully, however, I realized that he was singing only one word to the great old tune. The word was "Amen."

"Amen" was Andrew's church word for an as yet abbreviated religious vocabulary. But he was singing it with gusto, and in such a way as to make me realize that he knew the tune from some previous church exposure. He looked up at me with a distinct twinkle in his eye and his winning smile, and kept on singing.

"Amen" is faith's language of affirmation and promise. It is the word of hope and expectation affixed to our prayers. While never officially correct, only added by the tradition of the church, it is a time-honored ending to most of the great hymns. It is a grand declaration of authenticity to the mighty acts of God. It is our human word offering regarding God's greatest revelation.

Jesus is the centerpiece of all creation, the Master of the Way we are called to live, and our saving grace. He is the focus of the only truth that matters. He is the image of the invisible God and the image of truest humanity. Every promise God has made finds its yes in Him.

Keep singing your "Amen," Andrew. Sing that marvelous affirmation to every tune in the hymnbook. Sing it with your eyes, your lips, and with all your heart. Expressions of a living faith don't get any better than a simple "amen!"

# The Cycle Continues

> *As long as the earth endures, seedtime and harvest . . .*
> *summer and winter . . . shall not cease.*
> *(Genesis 8:22)*

Christmastide has come once again. The air is cold and crisp. Carefully placed garden mulch gives a protective coating to the precious soil, anticipating the hard freeze of January. Trees and plants stand dormant and seemingly lifeless.

Christmastide also means a brief sojourn south once again, and a celebrative visit with grandchildren and their parents. There will be a scramble for grandpa's lap to watch a particular seasonal video, and competitive requests for grandma to work a new Christmas puzzle. There will be stories and laughter and food and fun for a few exceptional days snatched from an otherwise busy and full calendar.

Somewhere in the midst of it all, the mail carrier will arrive with an important document—the ever-faithful seed catalog for another growing season. The grandchildren and I will review the "book" together. Matthew will once again make sure I have ordered lots of broccoli with cheese. Andrew will insist on cherry tomatoes—the kind he can snatch from the vine and pop directly into his mouth. Both boys will ask for cucumbers, for they dearly love sliced cucumber salad. Casey will not yet have enough experience to make her selection, but she will participate—never to be left out of such occasions. And a new grandchild, Luke, born during the late summer, will await his turn another Christmas week and another year.

The Christmas message recalls the glorious gift of a gracious God. The delivery of the seed catalog reminds us of a promise made to Noah long before the first Christmas. God covenants to be faithful. I want to covenant to be the kind of grandfather who reminds his grandchildren of that faithful God.

Images of love and life are readily seen in the lively faces of grandchildren and in the colorful promise of a seed catalog. May we always remember and give thanks for the bounty of God's grace in each one.

# About the Author

Brian K. Bauknight is senior pastor at Christ United Methodist Church in Bethel Park, Pennsylvania, and the author of *Gracious Imperatives*. He and his wife, Elaine, have four grown children and four growing grandchildren. Needless to say, his hobbies are gardening and grandchildren.